MW01268340

Black Panther for Kids - Learn Fun Facts about the Different Type of Black Panther Species in This Black Panther Book for Kids

Julie Walton

Magnificent Shadows

It will take a while for adventurers to came across this big cat. Aside for being quite quick and careful on their movements, they prefer to use their appearances as cloak or disguise whenever they hunt. They are like shadows next to a tree.

It's like a still figure waiting for its prey and if you are close enough, the only thing you can hear are the Black Panther's slow purring until they jump at their dinner and enjoy their hunt for the day. They look like magnificent shadows lurking alone in dark. And most of the time, no one knows that they are even there.

A Rare Specie?

They are, indeed, rare but they are not a separate kind of big cat. Species is a group or set of animals or plants that have the same characteristics and can breed with each other.

Funny as it sounds but Black Panther simply means big black cats. Although, we are not referring to small domestic black cats but big cats specifically jaguars and leopards.

Panthers

Panthera where the word 'Panther' came from means a classification of species like tigers, jaguars, lions and leopards. However, sadly, we don't have black tigers or lions. It would have been nice to came across a black lion.

Again, to end all speculations, black panther just simply means black leopards or jaguars. But what makes a black panther black? They tend stand out from the rest of their Panthera family that makes us wonder why it should be a separate specie.

It is all in the genes

The color of Black Panthers is due to Melanism. It is a dark-colored pigment in the skin called melanin that brings out a black or dark brown color to our eyes, hair and skin. And the same applies to Black Panthers, only in their case, it works on overdrive. There is an opposite of melanism called albinism which gives some animals that snowy white color.

Melanism can actually be an advantage and Black Panther does use it effectively for hunting. Perhaps their tactics are also passed on from generation to generation. That part, we'll never know for sure. What we know is that the dark-colored animals use their color as camouflage or cover-up.

Melanistic animals are more likely to survive in the jungle and are more likely to reproduce. Studies show that although Black Panthers are rare, there are a large number of these type of big cats from dense or thick forest around the globe. That is, if you can see them.

Black as Night

Now this is another misconception! Did you know that Black Panthers are not completely silky black? Adventurers, zoologists and animal biologists however, have been quite close to black panthers and discovered that these big cats also have spots!

Like other leopards and jaguars, Black Panthers also have the same prints. And some black panthers are not entirely black but dark brown.

Black leopards can give birth to both black and regular spotted leopards. But leopards can only produce regular spotted leopards. These also applies to jaguars.

The Three Continents

Black Panthers can be found in three continents. They embrace the dark this forest, the large trees near swamplands and tall grasslands where they can lay and watch the night sky. Panthers can be found in Asia, America and Africa.

Black Jaguars can be found under the deep rainforest of Central and South America. Black Leopards, on the other hand, prefer the wooded jungles or tropical forest of Africa and Asia. I wonder if they can come across cute and cuddly pandas in Asia. Oh wait, I hope not.

Home for Black Panthers!

Even large dominant mammals need their home and plays a vital role in the forest. Although there are three large continents where panthers live, they are close to being extinct. A lot of them are dying due to deforestation, illegal cutting of trees and illegal hunting of rare animals.

Both Leopards and Jaguars are endangered species, and that means their black brothers and sisters panthers are too. These days, Black Panthers rarely show themselves to humans at all, so it is a must that younger generations should know how to share their deep forest lands to our stealthy friend.

Thinking Glasses: On!

Let us set aside this chapter for some scientific facts! It is best to know a couple of terms and trivia to continue reading how Black Panther go on their adventure. Let's put on our thinking glasses, shall we?

Black Panthers are part of the class: Mammalia. They are also a part of the family classification of Felidae which means a family of cats. We also tackled this earlier, the genus or biological classification of Black Panthers is Panthera.

Not so bad, isn't it? The black Leopard's scientific name is Panthera Pardus while black Jaguars' scientific name is Panthera Onca.

The Coal Furred Loner

Even though Black Panthers are beautiful, they are a bit of a loner and tend to hunt, travel and spend most of their time alone. They don't form an alliance or create a pack like wolves. They like to observe their surroundings and perhaps enjoy its beauty on their own.

Then again, it is quite hard to sneak up on their prey if they hunt in groups. But how do Panther's reproduce? This big cat, however loner he or she may be, has a romantic side.

Knight in Shining Dark Fur

Black Panthers love their own company, but they do get lonely at times and that's where the fairytale comes in! At times, female Black Panthers will make a certain sound and mark a scent for their prince charming to find. A male Black Panther would follow the sound and track the scent to find his damsel, perhaps not in distress.

However, the mating season does not last for more than a few days and their fairytale will eventually come to an end.   A Black Panther usually looks for a partner and reaches maturity when they are two to three years old. They are then ready to mate and have cute cuddly baby panthers!

Raised by Queens

Their mothers alone raise baby Panthers. After mating, a lady Black Panther will be pregnant for three months and eventually produce two or four fuzzy cubs. By then, the male Black Panther would continue on his solitary adventure. Since Black Panthers are simply black Jaguars or Leopards, they can also produce regular spotted Jaguars and Leopards.

Black Panther cubs are very vulnerable and are blind during their first two weeks. Their mothers, having their queen-soldier-like attitude in the jungle, will have to look out for their litter babies and hunt for their food as well. Another fun fact! A group of panther cubs is referred as 'litters'.

Honestly, like human kids, they do tend to litter while playing and discovering their surroundings.

The Soldier Cubs

Panther cubs are witty and easily trained. After a few months, they will tag along with their mothers and help her take down their prey. A nine-month-old cub can also take down small preys on their own.

A litter of cubs will learn the ways of the jungle by simply following their mother and mimicking her hunting style. They will learn how hide like a shadow or swim and climb trees. Time would tell if each of them are ready to take on an adventure all on their own.

They Do Love Meat

As mentioned earlier, Black Panthers are mammals. Mammals are warm blooded, which means they can keep their bodies warm even when it is quite cold outside. This also helps black panthers adapt more on snowy, rainy or sunny seasons.

Mammals are also vertebrates, which mean they have a backbone that supports their body structure. Mammals also have hair on their bodies and can produce milk to feed their babies. Humans, on the other hand, can eat both meat and vegetables, while Black Panthers are carnivorous mammals, which means they only eat meat.

They like to eat vegetable-eating-animals like wild boars, rabbits, monkeys, deer or any mammals that might crossed their path so it is best to stay clear when you came across this cute but deadly creature.

Tarzan's Friend?

Have you watched Tarzan? I bet it is only a misunderstanding when he and that black panther got into a messy fight. Perhaps the Black Panther was just sad because they did not ask him to teach them how to climb trees. Yes, Black Panthers can climb trees!

In fact, one of their hunting tactic is to climb a tree, wait for them to come closer then pounce down at them using their big jaws of sharp teeth! Some Panthers usually sleeps on a large and low tree branch. They like their alone-time so they kept hidden on top of the tree while taking a long nap or spying nearby strangers.

Paw Splashes

I bet people rarely know this but Black Panthers love to swim too! They use their paws to paddle in deep water. No wonder other animals are terrified of Black Panthers. Their ability to swim and climb can be a disadvantage from a slow or injured animal who just wanted to take a stroll around the jungle!

Some Panthers who live in deep forests without open water may not know how to swim. Besides, if there are no swamps or lake to swim on how can they train? It is quite ideal to see big cat having fun swimming and splashing water using their cute paws, though.

Furry Vampires

One distinct characteristics of Black Panthers is that they are nocturnal. They prefer to hunt at night or at dusk. It is an advantage given that they are black as night.

They can be mistaken as a ghost or a shadow moving

slowly until they are right next to you with their gleaming fangs. Yikes! I thought I was describing a vampire. Like stated earlier, they use their melanistic color as an advantage that made them survive the laws of the jungle.

Panther's Journey

A Black Panther can live for twelve to fifteen years in the wild. They have mastered their ninja skills at a very young age and it is a definite that they have quite a few adventures to look back by the time they reached their fifteenth birthday!

Black Panthers are very strong and quite quick. They can jump up to twenty feet to capture their prey and can run up to thirty-five miles per hour. They are the ideal warrior and it would be a dream to see its journey up close!

Everyone's Dream Sidekick

Black Panthers are used in a lot of tales, movies and even as a sports team logo! Who could resist the characteristics of a ninja-like big cat, a shadow of the night appearance or its warrior-like ability? The very rarity of the animal makes it magical that could lead to stories waiting to be written.

If one could have a sidekick, a number of kids will raise their hands and shout a mighty Panther's roar! Who wouldn't want a guardian who's awake at night and can take down a monster hiding under your bed or inside your creaking closet? I bet an ebony furry companion sounds ideal now—that is if you can spot one.

Made in the USA
Lexington, KY
08 July 2019